A Midsummer Night's Dream

For Kids

T 7904

by
Lois Burdett

A Firefly Book

Copyright © 1997 Lois Burdett

Cataloguing in Publication Data

Burdett, Lois
    A midsummer night's dream for kids

(Shakespeare can be fun)
ISBN 1-55209-130-9 (bound)   ISBN 1-55209-124-4 (pbk.)

1. Children's plays, Canadian (English).* 2. Children's poetry, Canadian (English).* 3. Readers' theatre.
I. Shakespeare, William, 1564-1616. Midsummer night's dream.   II. Title.   III. Series.

PR2878.M5B87 1997   jC812'.54   C97-930415-6

Published by
Firefly Books Ltd.
3680 Victoria Park Avenue
Willowdale, Ontario
Canada M2H 3K1

Published in the U.S. by
Firefly Books (U.S.) Inc.
P.O. Box 1338, Ellicott Station
Buffalo, New York 14205

Printed and bound in Canada
by Friesens
Altona, Manitoba

Design production by
Fortunato Aglialoro
Falcom Design & Communications Inc

To my parents, who first introduced me to the magic of Shakespeare

Lois Burdett's Grade 2 students perform *A Midsummer Night's Dream* on the stage of the Festival Theatre for the professional cast in Stratford, Ontario. (From left) Back row: Brad Jesson (age 7) as Pyramus; Nicky Walch (age 7) as Thisbe. Front row: Ryan Flanagan (age 7) as Lysander; Alison Dickens (age 7) as Helena; Scott Burdett (age 7) as Demetrius.

Other books in the series:
A Child's Portrait of Shakespeare
Twelfth Night for Kids
Macbeth for Kids

Foreword

On a cold, snowy January day, my life changed. I was attending a conference of the Shakespeare Theatre Association of America, hosted by the Stratford Festival in Stratford, Ontario, Canada. As we sat discussing the future of classical repertory theatre, we were informed that we would be entertained by Lois Burdett and her second- and third-grade class from Hamlet School. The response to this announcement was polite silence. After all, we were important people who had flown an awfully long way to talk about art and theatre.

Then they arrived, these little people. Their teacher, Lois Burdett, introduced the play we were about to see, a piece called *A Child's Portrait of Shakespeare*. Mrs. Burdett then turned and faced the children, their eyes locked onto her like 25 pairs of lasers. She raised her arms, the children inhaled as one being, and with the skill of an accomplished symphonic conductor she struck a downbeat that unleashed such an energy surge that I felt the hair rise up on the back of my neck.

I'm told the performance lasted just under an hour. I couldn't tell you, because I was utterly transported. These little people had taken a room full of fairly cynical theatre folk and turned it upside down. Grown men were weeping and laughing in the same moment. And *not* because the performers were cute. Cute doesn't cut it in the professional theatre. No, there was something very special in what we witnessed that day.

I decided to invite Lois Burdett and the kids to perform their version of *Macbeth* at the Utah Shakespearean Festival that summer, where we too were performing the Scottish play. The week they spent here will live in the hearts and minds of all who had the good fortune to experience their visit. Every performance sold out, even in our biggest theatre of 1200 seats. Professional actors in attendance told me they felt they had been part of something powerful. Mrs. Burdett's workshops were inspiring, and teachers left with huge smiles on their lips and tears on their cheeks.

I wish all of you reading this book could meet Mrs. Burdett and her students. They know that the world says "kids can't do Shakespeare." But as you'll see for yourselves, in the pages of this book, they are more than happy to prove the world wrong. In this remarkable adaptation of *A Midsummer Night's Dream*, you will discover a world of possibilities.

So now – parents, teachers, and children – sit back and enjoy the wonder and magic of Shakespeare.

GARY ARMAGNAC
Director of Education, Utah Shakespearean Festival

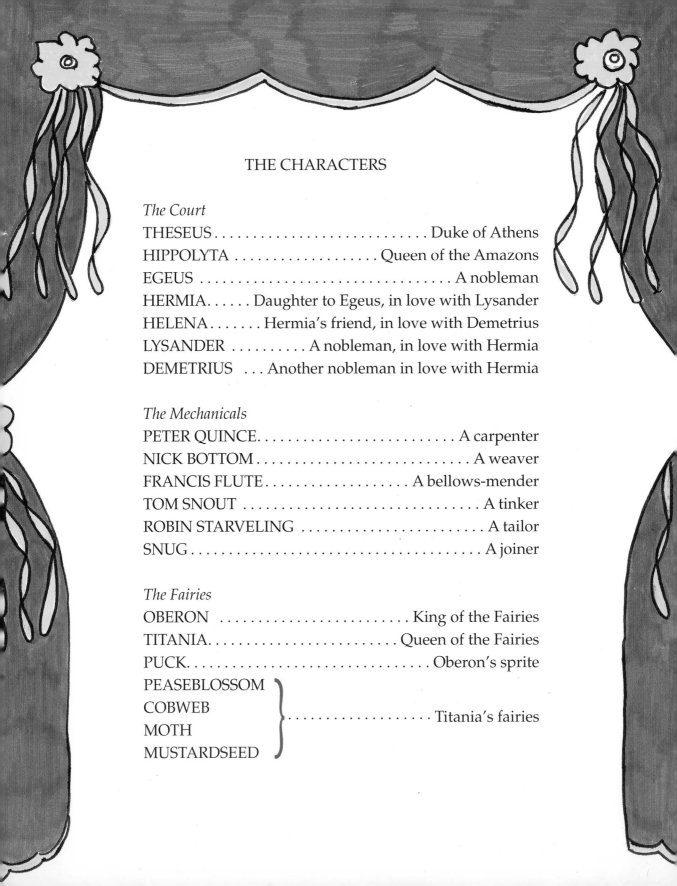

THE CHARACTERS

The Court

THESEUS . . . . Duke of Athens

HIPPOLYTA . . . . Queen of the Amazons

EGEUS . . . . A nobleman

HERMIA. . . . . . Daughter to Egeus, in love with Lysander

HELENA . . . . Hermia's friend, in love with Demetrius

LYSANDER . . . . A nobleman, in love with Hermia

DEMETRIUS . . . Another nobleman in love with Hermia

The Mechanicals

PETER QUINCE. . . . . A carpenter

NICK BOTTOM . . . . A weaver

FRANCIS FLUTE. . . . . A bellows-mender

TOM SNOUT . . . . A tinker

ROBIN STARVELING . . . . A tailor

SNUG . . . . A joiner

The Fairies

OBERON . . . . King of the Fairies

TITANIA. . . . . Queen of the Fairies

PUCK. . . . . Oberon's sprite

PEASEBLOSSOM
COBWEB . . . . Titania's fairies
MOTH
MUSTARDSEED

Dulcie Vousden (age 7)

I have a story, strange but true,
That I would like to share with you.
I set the stage to begin my show,
In Athens, Greece, so long ago.
Now let me take you back in time,
When a Duke named Theseus was in his prime ...

The Duke ruled Athens and was top in command;
He governed his people with a firm, steady hand.
A Queen, named Hippolyta, would soon share his life;
In just four days, they'd be husband and wife.
Throughout this great city, the excitement grew;
A huge feast was proposed. Entertainment, too!
These arrangements were made at a feverish rate,
But the business of governing would not wait.

Alex Fitzpatrick (age 7)

Kate Vanstone (age 10)

A man named Egeus burst into the room;
His face was furrowed with fury and gloom.
His daughter, Hermia, felt the strain;
She knew her father was there to complain.
A young lad, Lysander, followed behind;
Passionate love thoughts enveloped his mind.
He cherished dear Hermia, that was clear.
So did Demetrius, who brought up the rear.

Demetrius Lysander Hermia Egeus

Kimberly Brown (age 9)

7

Egeus bowed low to the Duke and confided,
"My daughter won't marry the one I decided.
Demetrius is the mate I chose,
Yet to this poor man she snubs her nose.
She wants to be Lysander's wife,
I won't allow it! Not on your life!
I tell you, Duke Theseus, this is the last straw.
I come to beg the power of the law.
She must do as I say and listen to me,
Or prepare to die; that is the decree!"

Egeus

In the olden days there was a stoopid law. Girls HAD to marry who ever their father picked or their heads would get chopped off their necks! Hermia's father didn't think Lysander was so hot. He ordered her to marry Demetrius.

Story: Alison Dickens (age 7)
Picture: Théa Pel (age 7)

8

The noble Duke rose from his lofty throne,
"Your behaviour, young lady, I cannot condone.
You're making your father very irate,
And on this matter, there will be no debate.
Fathers choose husbands! That is the rule!
So marry Demetrius. Don't be a fool!"
Poor Hermia pleaded in tragic despair;
She thought this rule was completely unfair.

Anika Johnson (age 7)

Hermia

Duke Theseus

"I despise Demetrius!" she said with candour,
"I am devoted to handsome Lysander.
This love in my heart cannot be swayed;
To marry another would be a charade."
The Duke was offended, "I said there's no choice.
You'll forfeit your life," he replied in a strong voice.
"Or in a convent spend the rest of your days.
You must decide soon. There will be no delays."
Hermia protested, "This law I defy!
I'll become a nun. I'll even die!"

Hermia

Dear Father,
I don't know what you see in that Demetrius. He's just a bug in a jug and a slug in a mug. Lysander makes my hart do a dance. He is two thumbs up. Oh Dad I love him and you will never convinse me to marry Demetrius.
    Sinserly your doter,
        Hermia

Story: Keshia Williams (age 7)
Picture: Elly Vousden (age 8)

The atmosphere was very tense.
Then Lysander spoke out in his own defence,
"I'm as rich as Demetrius and as well born.
Hermia's love for me, you must not scorn.
And furthermore, I wish to say,
Demetrius loved Helena until yesterday.
He courted the lady and won her soul,
I tell you, Demetrius has no self-control!"
The Duke interrupted, "I've heard of this talk!
I'll speak with him on it, but you'd better take stock.
The law of Athens cannot be denied;
By my wedding day, you'll have to decide."

Lysander

Dear Hermia,
I declare we will have no
more of this nonsens. Demetrius
is a perfectly fine fellow. In fact,
he is a downright genius in
my point of view, and should
be in yours too. Your performence
before the duke was discraseful.
Marrying Lysander is out of
the queschen. I hope this
letter will change your atitude.
          Your embarised father
                  Egeus
P.S. And don't try any funny
bisness!

Anika Johnson (age 7)

Carolyn Parr (age 9)

11

The Duke and his group then quickly departed;
Hermia was desolate and broken-hearted.
"Don't cry!" said Lysander. "Your tears I will soothe,
For the course of true love never did run smooth.
An aunt of mine lives seven leagues away;
We could go to her place without delay.
She has no children, not even one;
She loves me as though I were her son.
There we shall marry and end this sorrow;
Run away with me, at twilight tomorrow."

My dearest Hermia,
If I had my pick of all the girls in the galicksee you would be the one I would choose. I adore you Hermia. I trooly do. Tomorrow night we will stow away into the woods. We'll go to my aunt's home and there we will be wedded. But remember this is top secret. Do not, I repeat DO NOT let your father see this letter.
     Your adorabull Lysander
P.S. My darling you take my breth away!

Matt Doughty (age 7)

Anika Johnson (age 7)

12

Hermia, whose face was tear-stained and pale,
Glowed with new hope, "I will not fail!"
Lysander, I vow by Cupid's bow,
Tomorrow night, I'll be ready to go.
"We'll meet in the forest," she said without fear,
"Then into the darkness we'll disappear.
Together, my dear, we both shall flee,
And at your aunt's home, I'll marry thee!
My sweet Lysander, I will no longer grieve."
Then they kissed good-bye and turned to leave.

Dearest Lysander,
Yes I will meet with you.
I am in such desperat need
of you. Lysander you are like
a fluffy white cloud on a
sunny day. Demetrius is the
thunder. I shiver with delite
when you walk down the
road. You know I do not
want my head chopped off.
That would not be a pretty
picture!
　　　　　　　Hermia

Morgan Pel (age 8)

Robyn Lafontaine (age 7)

13

They hadn't taken but a single pace,
When the two were greeted by a familiar face.
It was Helena, Hermia's best friend;
It looked like she was at her wit's end.
"Hermia," she sighed, "Demetrius is my life,
But he dotes on you. I'll never be his wife.
Oh teach me, Hermia. Tell me what to do.
If only I were as beautiful as you."
Hermia replied, "Dear Helena, don't cry.
I guarantee you, I can't stand your guy!
I frown on him coldly, yet he loves me still.
I love Lysander and I always will!"

Dear Diary,
I love Demetrius terably! But he will
have nothing to do with me. My hart
is full of misery. In return for all
my efferts to please him, he looks on
me coldly. Demetrius used to love me
but then he just dumped me.
If he ever cast a smile in my
direcshon, my hart would fly out
of my mouth. But right now it is
slithering along the floor, bursting
with sorrow. I feel like an old
hag. It is a tragic time!
                              Helena

Story: Anika Johnson (age 7)
Picture: Amber Roberts (age 10)

Helena

14

Then Lysander spoke out, he was gracious and kind,
"I'll tell you, dear friend, what's on my mind.
We're running away tomorrow night;
It's the only way to solve our plight!"
With that, the two left, content as could be.
Poor Helena was in agony.
"Demetrius loves Hermia!" she cried in despair.
"This is far more than I can bear!
How can I get him to love me instead?"
Then a brilliant idea crept into her head,
"I'll tell Demetrius of their scheme;
He'll thank me for sure, then I'll be supreme!"
So off she ran, her heart on fire,
To find Demetrius, her life-long desire.

Lysander

Secret Plan of Escape

1. Meet at the old razbury bush near the pond.

2. Be there at 9:07 P.M. on the dot.

3. We will need walking shoes and a candle to light our way.

4. Take food supplies (two of the basic food groups)

5. Pack a cantene of water, a toothbrush and a pillow to rest our heads.

6. Don't forget bandages for our blisters.

7. Bring all your money

8. Don't be late.

Glenn Truelove (age 8)

Dulcie Vousden (age 8)

Now all this time, not far away,
Six jolly men were practising a play.
Nick Bottom was there, and so was Tom Snout.
Robin Starveling, the tailor, was also about.
Francis Flute and Snug added to the din,
Then Peter Quince called, "We'd better begin!
A play's been requested for Theseus and his bride;
We haven't much time," Peter Quince cried.
"Their wedding is soon, so we'll have to act fast.
Now listen, as I read out the names of the cast."

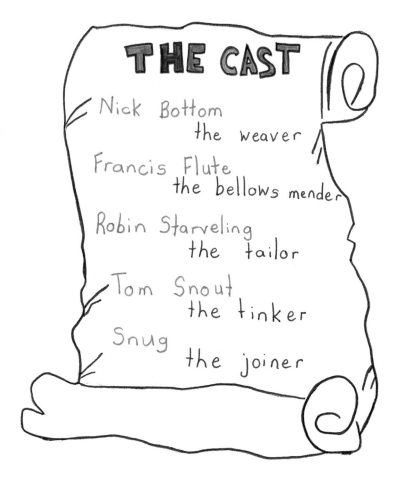

THE CAST

Nick Bottom
the weaver

Francis Flute
the bellows mender

Robin Starveling
the tailor

Tom Snout
the tinker

Snug
the joiner

Katie Carroll (age 7)

Peter Quince

Ashley Kropf (age 10)

16

"Nick Bottom, the weaver, your role is to be
Pyramus, a lover, as you will soon see.
A lover most gallant that kills himself for love."
Nick was ecstatic. The role fit like a glove.
"A lover!" he cried, "It's such a great part.
I'll give the ladies a change of heart!
I'll have them all in showers of tears.
They'll remember my acting for many years.
My Pyramus will be hard to resist.
But proceed, dear Quince, go on with your list."

Acting Tips
by Nick Bottom

1. Don't trip on your toes.

2. Don't slop food on your costume.

3. Don't get the hicups.

4. Don't fall asleep.

5. Don't tumble down the trap door.

6. Don't really brake a leg.

7. Don't forget to come.

Nick Bottom

Story: David Marklevitz (age 8)
Picture: Ashley Kropf (age 10)

17

"Francis Flute, you'll take Thisbe's role;
I want you to give it your heart and soul."
Flute was excited; his eyes sparkled bright,
"What is Thisbe?" he asked, "A wandering knight?"
"Oh, no," Quince replied, "Thisbe's a she,
And madly in love with Pyramus, you see."
"I'll not play a woman," Francis Flute sneered,
"Can't you see I've started a beard?"
"Let me be Thisbe," Bottom shouted with joy,
"I'll be the girl as well as the boy.
I can speak like a lady. I'll be sweet as a dove.
'Oh, Pyramus,'" he chirped, "'You are my love.'"
"No way!" Quince shouted, "You'll be the guy.
I'm the director, and you must comply."

Francis Flute

Jacqueline Parr (age 9)

Snug

Jeremiah Courtney (age 9)

Then Quince turned to Snug, "In our tale of woe,
You'll be the lion in our show."
"I'll need the script now!" Snug said with concern,
"It'll take me quite a while to learn.
For I'm slow of study, I implore!"
"Don't worry," cried Quince, "All you do is roar!"

18

Nick Bottom jumped up and down with glee,
"That fiercesome beast, I could be!
I'd growl so loud, they would never complain,
They'd beg me to do it, again and again!
Roar!" he thundered, then his tone became smug,
"I told you, I'm much better than Snug!"
"You'd scare the ladies," Quince said, "and that's wrong!"
"Then I will roar soft as a nightingale's song.
Roar, roar," Bottom started to squeak,
"I know the women will love my technique."
"You're Pyramus!" Quince cried, "That ends the debate!
Any more of this talk, I'll not tolerate!
We'll meet in the woods tomorrow night,
And rehearse our play by the moon's silver light."

Erin Bick (age 10)

19

The hours dragged on till the following eve;
The four desperate lovers prepared to leave.
Lysander and Hermia met as was planned,
Then trudged through the forest, hand clutching hand.
Demetrius followed the couple's route;
Helena chased after in hot pursuit.
They all moved through the woods unknown,
But these mortals were not alone.

Helena

Demetrius

Eliza Johnson (age 7)

Lysander Hermia

And if they'd looked closely and listened with care,
They'd have heard rustling in the bushes out there.
Perhaps they'd have seen the shimmer of wings,
And many other magical things.
For in the dark woods, as the humans took flight,
The fairies held revels far into the night.
Oberon was King of this fairy land,
And the little sprites jumped to his every command.

Ashley Kropf (age 10)

But for fairies, too, life's not always serene;
Oberon had quarrelled with Titania, his Queen.
"Ill met by moonlight, proud Titania," he said.
The Queen paused as her fairies fled.
"Why are you here?" she cried in disdain.
"All you do is argue and complain!
Since the start of midsummer, we've had this feud;
It's put all nature in an angry mood!"
"Then change it," he cried, "You have the cure;
Your stubbornness I'll not endure!
Fill your Oberon's heart with joy;
I do but beg your servant boy.
Come now, Titania, it's my only request.
He'll be my helper, and we'll end this unrest."

Oberon

Titania,
I am your husband and you know wives and husbands always share. I am in frantic need of your servant boy. I'll give you my whole kingdum and everything your hart dezires. Please! please! with two wings on top and a tuch of sparcle dust. I'll get down on my hands and knees if that's what it takes.
Oberon

Laura Bates (age 7)

Sophie Jones (age 8)

Titania's anger was acute,
"It's not that easy to end our dispute.
You do not seem to comprehend;
This boy is the son of a very dear friend.
She was in my service," Titania said with a sigh,
"But alas, she was human, and had to die.
I promised her I'd raise her son,
And I won't give him to anyone.
The fairy land buys not the child of me.
Come hither, my elves. Away we shall flee!"

Titania

Oberon
No matter how you plead I'm keeping the boy. You could give me the universe and it wouldn't do any good. We both know you have more than enuf servants. And what's more to feed him, chase him and clean up after him... ...Well that is too much for you to handle. Oberon, you don't always have to get your own way. For the last time the boy stays here.
                    Your very agravated
                    Titania

Story: Katie Carroll (age 8)
Picture: Sophie Jones (age 8)

23

Then Titania left with her fairy lot.
"I'll get my revenge," Oberon thought.
"But I'll need some help to change my bad luck,"
So he called for his sprite, a fairy named Puck.
Robin Goodfellow was Puck's real name;
In the world of magic, he held much acclaim.
For Puck was always playing jokes
On all the unsuspecting folks.
But this was not a time for glee,
As the fairy king began his plea:
"I need you to find an unusual flower.
I'm in frantic need of its magical power.
It's called love-in-idleness, my little sprite;
It's purple in colour, though it used to be white.
When sleeping eyes are streaked with its juice,
A powerful love potion is set loose."

Puck

Erin Bick (age 9)

Little Puck is about the size of my thumb. But he can do enormus tricks. In fact he has duzins up his sleeve. If there was a contest for jokes Puck would definetly win the champeonship.

Rebecca Courtney (age 7)

24

Oberon snickered, "I'll repay my Queen.
I'll observe her sleep in the forest green.
Then drop the nectar into her eyes;
When Titania awakens, she'll have a surprise.
The next thing she sees, be it bull, wolf, or bear,
She will suddenly feel a love most rare.
I will not cancel this magic spell,
Till she gives me the boy. Then all will be well."
Puck bowed to his King, "This flower I'll find,
I can do it so fast, it will boggle your mind!
I'll search everywhere and try hard to please!"
Then Puck fluttered off into the breeze.

Oberon

Now Puck my little trusted advizer. Look far and wide in serch of the flower...Not just any flower, the flower of love. Here is the discripshon. It's petels bloom with many colours of the rainbow. It smells like fresh mint and cinamin. Its necter shines in the sunlight and its pollen sprinkles like a gentle rain on a summer day. Puck I am counting on you and only you. Do not fail!

Laura Bates (age 7)

Dulcie Vousden (age 8)

As Oberon revelled in his spiteful scheme,
Demetrius raced in on another theme.
Helena followed a few steps behind,
"I pray you, my darling, change your mind.
I have, to you, my love unfurled,
For you, Demetrius, are all my world.
I reported their plan. I did my part.
I beg of you now, give me your heart!"

D-ear D-ear De-m-etrius
It is your pity that keeps
me alive each day. I am
on my hands and knees
for you. Your smile is so
glameris, it makes your
dimples lite up. You SPARKLE
and SHINE in the cool breeze.
  Your most afecShonit
    Helena

Ellen Stuart (age 8)

Dear   Demetrius
You are my only love. When I
see you I hold my breth
hoping that you will give me
a tender glance. You are
all that I live for! My hart
beats outrageusly fast when you
walk by! Everything about you
is perfect. When I am near you
I feel as if I'm dancing across
the sky! None in the world could
replace you!
          Your love bird
            Helena

Anika Johnson (age 7)

Caitlin More (age 11)

26

Demetrius erupted like a raging cyclone,
"Get out of my life! Leave me alone!
I told you before, you make me ill.
I love Hermia and I always will!"
By now, poor Helena was completely distraught,
"He'll change his mind," she desperately thought.
Demetrius stomped off, "It's Hermia I must find."
Helena sobbed and ran along behind.

Dear Helena
Helena did you know that you are dispikabull, absulootly dispikabull! Helena I don't even like you. Achualy I hate you. Get out of my life and I mean it! If you follow me again I will do all the things I described! get lost from Demetrius

Demetrius

Story: Julian Smith (age 7)
Picture: Adam Robinson (age 8)

27

Now Oberon was touched by Helena's plight,
So he made a second promise that night.
"This shameful conduct just won't do.
I'll use the flower on this lad, too!
When the young man awakes, he'll see Helena's face,
And it will be her, he'll want to embrace."
Then the fairy king searched the skies for his sprite,
"When Puck returns, we'll make everything right."

The flower of romance is nowhere to be found. I have looked in the United States and in Switzerland but no luck. I didn't even find a trail of love dust. One secind I am steaming hot in the muggy air over Egypt and then in a flash I'm uterly cold and chilled over Norway. I must not give up my serch. But I can tell you I am one eggzosted little fairy.
Puck (Otherwise known as Robin Goodfellow)

Story: Katie Carroll (age 8)
Picture: Julie Wilhelm (age 9)

Oberon

28

Meanwhile, little Puck continued his probe;
He looked like a blur, as he circled the globe.
Finally, in a distant place,
Puck found the flower to end the chase.
It smelled like sweet honey and had a soft touch.
He cradled it gently, it was treasured so much.
Then homeward bound, he blazed through the night,
Soaring at the speed of light.

Katie Brown (age 8)

"Welcome, wanderer!" Oberon cried, "Well done!
We'll do our tricks now, one by one.
I know a bank where the wild thyme blows,
Where oxlips and the nodding violet grows.
There sleeps Titania some time of the night,
Lulled in these flowers with dances and delight.
I'll meet Titania for our rendezvous.
This juice will make all my dreams come true."

Story: Glenn Truelove (age 8)
Picture: Jeremiah Courtney (age 9)

There it was... the flower I had been serching for. I swooped down at ramming speed. This flower is like a tree to us pixsees and it will be tuff to chop it down. But I can't work on an empty stumic. I pulled out my picnic basket and ate chunks of olive and bread crumbs and drank a thimble full of lemunade. Then I took a mighty swing and the flower was mine!

Oberon continued, "And you, my comrade!
Must find the youth who's gone stark raving mad.
The lady he scorns follows close behind;
You must give this Demetrius a change of mind.
Take some of this juice and anoint his eyes,
But make sure Helena's the first one he spies.
You'll know the lad by his Athenian clothes.
Come back before the rooster crows."
"Fear not," Puck replied, "I'll do as you ask!"
Then off he flew to complete the task.

PUCK

Oberon

Sophie Jones (age 8)

But Puck was soon to commit a blunder.
He'd mix up the couples, and that was no wonder.
Hermia and Lysander still wandered around,
The home of his aunt was nowhere to be found.
The gentle Hermia was most distressed,
"Beloved, I'm faint. I need to rest!
Lysander find you out a bed,
For I upon this bank will rest my head.
It would be wrong, if together we'd stay."
So Lysander lay down, a short distance away.

Rebecca Courtney (age 8)

Dearest Lysander
My feet are killing me.
I know we want to get
to your aunt's home but
I am sweetly saying that
I am fed up with walking.
My legs feel like mashed
potatoes and we're being
eaten alive by mosquitoes.
This forest goes on forever!
Hermia

Erin Bick (age 9)

Above the forest, eager Puck flew,
Until this twosome came into his view.
"There is the youth, that Oberon chose,
For he is wearing just the right clothes.
And here is the maiden, sleeping sound,
On the dank and dirty ground.
They lie apart, another good sign,
His romantic intentions, I'll realign.
A powerful passion, I will induce."
On Lysander's eyes, Puck poured the charmed juice.
"So awake when I am gone.
For I must now to Oberon!"

Tiffany Foster (age 10)

Along came Helena, gasping for air;
Her heart was heavy and full of despair,
"Oh I am out of breath in this fond chase,
The more my prayer, the lesser is my grace."
She saw Lysander lying in a heap,
And rushed to him, "Is he dead or asleep?
Lysander if you live, good sir, awake…"
"…And run through fire I will for thy sweet sake,"
Replied Lysander as he leapt to his feet,
Embracing Helena, "You are my sweet!"

Dulcie Vousden (age 7)

Dearest Helena,
My heart bleeds for you.
Your rose-bud lips, your dark
soft hair, your beautiful smooth
face and hands are just
perfect for me. I am in a
deep love spell for you. Your
eyes are like sparkling ice,
shimering over me. You are
all my dreams come true!
                    Lysander

Ashley Kropf (age 10)

34

"You've got to be kidding!" Helena cried,"
I know, it's Hermia, you want for your bride."
"Not a chance!" said Lysander, "It's you I love!
Who will not change a raven for a dove?"
"Give me a break!" Helena scoffed in dismay,
"Do you think I was born yesterday?
Your speech to me is like a thorn;
How dare you treat me with such scorn!"
Then she stomped off, in great disdain;
Lysander followed with a loving refrain.

Dear Lysander
You've been in the sun too long! I know you dote on Hermia and you always will. How dare you treat me like this. If you think I will stand for this nonsints any longer you are dredfully mistaken!
Your much annoyed
Helena

Morgan Pel (age 8)

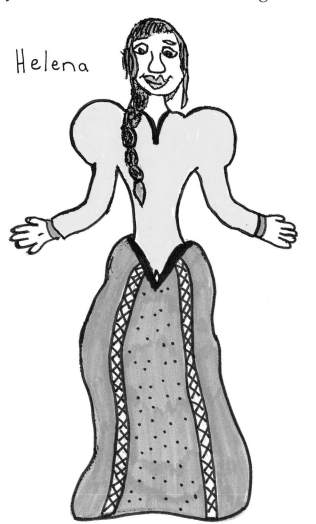

Helena

Tiffany Foster (age 10)

Lysander

But what about Hermia, still sound asleep,
Lying on the grass in a curled-up heap?
Soon she awoke from a dreadful nightmare;
She couldn't find Lysander anywhere.
"Lysander, my love, what has occurred?
Out of hearing? Gone? No sound? No word?
Alack, where are you? Speak if you can!"
Then into the night, she ran after her man.

This is the sadest day of my life. My hart sinks low. It is a night mare come troo!

Picture: Nika Mistruzzi (age 10)
Caption: Jeff Brown (age 7)

As Hermia awoke from her slumber deep,
Titania, the fairy queen, wanted to sleep.
She called to her fairies who were playing nearby,
"I need you to sing me a lullaby."
Peaseblossom and Moth were the first to begin,
Then Cobweb and Mustardseed joined right in.
They circled Titania, who made not a peep.
For she had fallen fast asleep.

Megan Vandersleen (age 9)

Oberon peered from behind the trees,
Then crept towards her on bended knees,
"What thou see'st when thou dost wake,
Do it for thy true-love take;
Be it lynx or cat or bear,
Leopard, or boar with bristled hair,
When thou wak'st, it is thy dear.
Wake when some vile thing is near."

Anika Johnson (age 7)

As chance would have it, quite near where she lay,
The six merry men were practising the play.
Not one of them noticed Puck appear,
For he was invisible and had nothing to fear.
Puck fluttered down from the air,
And hid behind the director's chair.
Then Bottom stood up to practise his cue;
He wanted to be ready for his debut.
As he left the stage, Puck followed behind,
A cunning thought brewing in his mind.
He'd work his magic on this man, too,
"I've the perfect idea what to do!"

Megan Vandersleen (age 9)

What followed next was hard to conceive;
His friends saw a sight they could not believe.
When Bottom returned, he had a new head,
No longer a man's, but a donkey's instead!
They all trembled with fear and stared at his face,
"Oh monstrous! Oh strange! Let us fly this place!"
The scene that followed was complete disarray;
They howled in terror, and all ran away.
Nick Bottom looked puzzled, "Why did they flee?
This is to make an ass of me!
I'll show them that I have no fear,
I'll march and sing out, loud and clear."

Peter Quince's Diary
I was just minding my own
bisness directing the play
when onto the stage
clomped a DONKEY!!!
I was red eyed shoked.
H-h-h-h-h-h-help! I
trembled in fear. I leapt
into the air in amazement
and then I ran like the
wind!

Sean McGarry (age 7)

Brad Jesson (age 7)

40

Titania was sleeping in her flowery bed,
When Bottom appeared, his arms outspread,
"Hee haw! Hee haw!" was his ludicrous tune.
Her eyes flew open. She wanted to swoon,
"Mine ear is much enamoured of thy strain.
I pray thee gentle mortal, sing again.
I am enchanted by your lovely notes;
Come, fairy servants, bring him some oats."
She wrapped sweet roses in his hair,
"You are beautiful, beyond compare!
Stay with me forever, I propose."
And then she kissed his soft, wet nose.

Nathan Rollerman (age 10)

Ears of silk
Head of brown
Soft melting eyes
Staring down
Reaching arms
Shoulders broad
Fur like cotton
A creature of God

Laura Bates (age 7)

41

Puck was delighted with the success of his plan,
And left Nick Bottom, part burro, part man.
Back to his master, he flew in a dash,
Intent to deliver the latest news flash.
Oberon was eager to hear of the trick,
"How did it go, Puck? Who did she pick?"
"Wait till I tell you," Puck said with pride,
"I know you will be satisfied!
She's in love with a monster," was Puck's report.
"A donkey!" he cried, "to make a long story short."
Oberon chuckled, "What a surprise!
This falls out better than I could devise."

I absolootly think Puck should not pull this trick. How would you like it if you had a nose six times bigger than your normel one?

Julian Hacquebard (age 7)

Tyler Preston (age 7)

Then they heard footsteps approaching their spot;
Hermia rushed in looking quite distraught.
Demetrius followed of his own free will,
"I won't give you up! I love you still!"
"Demetrius," she cried, "you're such a creep!
Did you kill Lysander while he was asleep?"
"I tell you I'm innocent!" Demetrius said,
"I'm sure Lysander is not dead!
Why do you scold me so severely?
My only fault is to love you dearly!"
"Demetrius, I know you speak in jest."
Hermia kept running. He lay down to rest.

Demetrius

Hermia

Robyn Lafontaine (age 7)

Carolyn Parr (age 9)

Oberon watched this scene in dismay,
And pointed to Demetrius in a worried way.
"Did you squeeze the juice into his eyes?
Tell me, Puck? And I want no lies."
"I remember the woman," Puck was alarmed,
"But that is not the man I charmed."
"Puck, oh Puck, this isn't right,
You chose the wrong man, you silly sprite!
Fly like the wind. Be Helena's guide.
Entice her back here, by this man's side.
Go quickly, Puck, and fix this mistake.
I'll use the flower to cure this heartache."

Puck had made a dredful
BOO-BOO! He put the love
juice into Lysander's eyes.
Helena came blubering by
with a pudel of tears
behind her. Lysander saw
Helena and fell in love.
Hermia is left with a
cracked up heart!
That makes confewshun!

Alison Dickens (age 7)

Caitlin More (age 11)

44

Oberon advanced and held out the bloom;
Demetrius inhaled its enchanting perfume.
As the fragrant potion shrouded his mind,
Puck appeared with Helena behind,
"Oh Captain, your wishes I did execute,
But Lysander is in swift pursuit!"
"Stand aside!" Oberon shouted, "This noise they make
Will cause Demetrius to awake!"
"Then," Puck grinned, "two will woo one,
And the sport will have just begun.
Shall we their fond pageant see?
Lord, what fools these mortals be!"

Oberon

Demetrius

Stephen Marklevitz (age 11)

Lysander,
Is this a cruel trick or what? You and Hermia love each other. Everyone knows that. So how could you love me? For your informashin, you're acting like you're from another planet. This is nuts around here!
                    Helena

Katie Carroll (age 7)

45

As Oberon and Puck quickly withdrew,
Lysander and Helena rushed into view.
"Helena," cried Lysander, "I worship you so!"
"You mock me," she yelled, "I told you to go!"
Then Demetrius awoke, "Oh Helena, divine!
Tell me you love me. Just give me a sign."
Then both of the men dropped to their knees,
And cried together, "Marry me please!"
Helena couldn't believe her ears,
Appalled to hear their taunting jeers,
"The two of you are acting absurd;
In fact, abnormal is the word!"

Helena

Ashley Kropf (age 10)

Demetrius cried, "I'll restart my life,
I must have Helena for my wife!"
Lysander countered, "It's me she adores.
My affection for her is greater than yours.
I'll prove it with the blade of my sword!"
This was a challenge that couldn't be ignored.
Helena watched in sheer disgust;
Neither of them had won her trust.
"Oh, spite, I see you all are bent
To set against me for your merriment.
If you were men, as men you are in show,
You would not use a gentle lady so."

Robbie Kew (age 8)

A Challenge
To Demetrius
I've had it up to my ears
with you. You're a pure
bread POACHER! Ya hear me
D-e-m-e-t-r-i-u-s! You really
burn me up the way
you whisper sweet
nothings into Helena's
ear! So THAT DOES
IT! I challenge you to
a fight 12 o'clock
midnight SPOT ON
THE DOT! Signed
Lysander

Ian Ferguson (age 9)

Dear Lysander
I'm the one Helena loves so go
and stop your bragging!! Do you
challenge me to a fight? If you don't
you're a mouse!!! The fight will be
jaw to jaw with madness. Besides you're
not as handsome as me. You should
just marry Hermia and be satisfied.
I'll give you some advise. Pack your
bags and get out! I love Helena
and nobody is going to stop me.
Your enemy Demetrius

Jeremy Thiel (age 8)

Now all of this caused quite a hullabaloo.
Hermia stumbled in, her clothes askew.
Her eyes were still wet; her head was hung low.
To lose Lysander had been a real blow.
Then out of the blue, she heard his voice;
She wasn't aware of his new love choice.
"Lysander," she smiled, "why did you go?"
"Behold," he replied, "It's the ugly old crow!"
Hermia could hardly believe her ears;
This was beyond her wildest fears.
"Is this a dream? It cannot be."
Lysander sneered, "It's Helena, for me."

Dear Diary,
When I last woke Lysander was gone! I don't know why he left me! So I stumbled into the darkness serching for him without success. Then I came to a clearing. And there, right in front of me stood Lysander, his arms wraped around Helena. Well this was too much for me. I stormed in to find out what in the world was going on...
Hermia

Hermia

Anika Johnson (age 7)

Robyn Lafontaine (age 7)

48

Helena's heart and mind were in a blur,
She thought they all made fun of her.
She turned on Hermia with passion deep,
"This game you play is really cheap!
Injurious Hermia, I do contend,
You join these men in scorning your poor friend."
Hermia was shocked, "You are the thief!
Your accusation defies belief!
Lysander is mine. You stole him by night.
You canker-blossom! You parasite!"
She lunged at Helena, "You painted maypole!"
The whole situation was soon out of control.

Helena

Ashley Kropf (age 10)

Helena,
Helena you listen and you listen up good, you double-crossing boyfriend snacher! Lysander is mine so hands off, as in don't tuch! You have lots of guys to pick from so why steal mine?
Your much annoyed
ex-best friend
Hermia

Katie Carroll (age 8)

49

Now Oberon looked on and saw his bad luck,
"You must stop this brawling," he told little Puck.
"This is your mess, so make everything right!
Hurry now, Puck. Overcast the night!"
The sprite obeyed his master's bid,
And in the forest quickly hid.
He directed the mortals round and round,
Until one by one, they collapsed on the ground.
Then he sprinkled the juice, as told to do,
In Lysander's eyes, and off he flew.

Lysander

Caitlin More (age 11)

There the four slept; the earth was their bed.
In came Titania, caressing Nick's head.
Nick brayed with pleasure in her embrace,
And his heart beat at a rapid pace.
The king of shadows watched from afar.
This was indeed a sight bizarre:
His lady wrapped in a donkey's arms,
Completely entranced by the creature's charms.
Oberon knew he'd done his Queen wrong,
And this silly behaviour he wouldn't prolong.
So he crept closer to Titania unseen,
And removed the spell from the eyes of his Queen.

A shimmering face
full of love
A voice like an angel
from above
You are the beauty
of my life
To comfort me
in joy or strife
Always shall
I treasure thee
And forever more
my sweetheart be.
     Titania

Anika Johnson (age 7)

Eliza Johnson (age 7)

51

Her eyes flew open, as if on cue,
And there sat Oberon in her view.
"Oh what visions have come to pass,
In one I dreamt I loved an ass!"
"There he lies sleeping," Oberon said,
"A wreath of flowers around his head."
Titania was shocked, "I loathe his face!
How could I worship a creature so base?"
Oberon suggested, "To the Duke's we'll retreat."
He whispered to Puck, "Get this clod on his feet!
Return the man's head. Send him back to his team.
Make him think it's all been a dream."

Julie Wilhelm (age 9)

With a hint of a smile and a twinkle in his eye,
Puck changed the donkey back into the guy!
Nick Bottom stood up; his vision seemed blurred,
He wondered aloud what had occurred,
"I have had a dream most rare!
So strange that it is hard to share.
I'll have Peter Quince write a song,
And I will sing it, loud and strong.
But now I think I should away,
To tell my friends and rehearse the play."

Nick Bottom

You won't beleeve the dream I had. I was part man part mule. It felt so real! I was just singing my fury head off when a fairy Queen cuddled up to me. She served me as only Queen's can. First she gave me a magnifusunt smooch. Then she dropped grapes in my mouth. I felt like a prince.

Matt Hunt (age 7)

Ashley Kropf (age 10)

53

Now all this time, the lovers were asleep,
Perfectly still, not making a peep.
At dawn, there entered in the glen,
Duke Theseus, Egeus, and their huntsmen.
They blew their trumpets, loud and clear.
The couples leapt to their feet, pale with fear.
Theseus demanded, "I'd like to know,
Were you not rivals, a short time ago?"

Duke Theseus

Sophie Jones (age 8)

Lysander spoke first, "I beseech your grace,
I am amazed at what took place.
It was with Hermia I ran away,
For the law of Athens, we would not obey.
In a dream I loved Helena, but not anymore.
Hermia's mine, as she was before."
Hermia's father was not amused,
Then Demetrius spoke out, just as confused,
"My love for Hermia has melted like snow.
It is to Helena, my heart I owe!"
Duke Theseus smiled, "I decree,
Instead of one wedding, we'll have three."

Elly Vousden (age 8)

Later, when their vows were done,
There was singing and dancing and lots of fun!
The Duke proclaimed, "And now for a play,
To celebrate our wedding day.
I'm told that it is tragical mirth.
We'll enjoy it for what it's worth."
"I am the Prologue!" Peter Quince cried.
"We don't want the ladies horrified.
So I'll tell you the story, blow by blow."
"What's this?" the Duke cried, "a one-man show?
Tis the silliest stuff I can recall,
Oh look, here comes the wall."

The Most Lamentable Comedy and Most Cruel Death of Pyramus and Thisbe

Shawn Koehler (age 10)

"In this play," said the tinker, "it doth befall,
That I, one Snout by name, present a wall!
And such a wall, as I would have you think,
That had in it a crannied hole, or chink.
Pyramus and Thisbe, the lovers in our play,
Whisper through me everyday."
Pyramus entered, "Oh sweet, oh lovely wall,
Show me the opening, so small."
Snout held up his fingers to make the crack,"
Thanks, courteous wall. Will Thisbe come back?"
Then Thisbe arrived, "Oh wall, hear my moans,
My cherry lips have often kissed thy stones."
"I see a voice!" Pyramus peered through the hole,
"Run away with me, Thisbe! You are my soul!
At Ninny's tomb, we'll meet straightaway."
"I'll come to you, Pyramus, without delay!"

Elly Vousden (age 8)

Then Starveling marched to centre stage,
Holding up his lighted cage.
"This lantern doth present the moon.
I wonder if Thisbe will get here soon?"
Starveling moved aside as Thisbe drew near.
A lion roared! She cried in fear,
"Pyramus, save me!" Thisbe said.
Her scarf flew off, as she quickly fled.
The lion grabbed it in his paws,
Then ripped it in his bloody jaws.
He roared again as he shook his prey,
Then dropped the cloth and lumbered away.

Ashley Kropf (age 10)

Pyramus arrived and saw the shred,
"Oh, my Thisbe. You can't be dead!
What, stained with blood?" he cried in pain,
"Oh dainty duck. Come back again!
I can't go on without you, dear.
My life is over! I'll end it here!"
He drew his sword, "I'm so distressed!"
Then thrust it deeply into his chest.
"I'm dying! I'm dying!" he cried aloud,
He listened to hear the cheers from the crowd.
"My pulse is ebbing!" Pyramus said.
He collapsed on the ground, and moaned, "I'm dead!"'

Will I ever see my little dumpling again? She was the cherry on my pie. She was the sprinkls on my ice cream. I cannot go on living without her. Good-bye grass! Good-bye flowers! Good-bye world! My life is history!
            Pyramus

Rebecca Courtney (age 7)

Amy Robinson (age 9)

Thisbe returned and let out a scream.
She staggered back, "Is this a dream?
Asleep my love?
What, dead, my dove?
These lily lips, this cherry nose,
These yellow cheeks, no longer rose,
Are gone! Are gone!
His sword is drawn!
Come trusty blade, my breast imbue,
And farewell friends! Adieu! Adieu!"

Pyramus my hunybun. Where are you? Oh there you are! Having a nap are you? What? Oh mizery...I hear no breathing! Pyramus speak to me! Are you dead or alive? Oh my little buttercup! You've gone and killed yourself haven't you? Farewell I die for thee!

David Marklevitz (age 8)

Sophie Jones (age 8)

And with these words the play was complete.
The crowd all clapped. They'd had a real treat!
The Duke proclaimed, "We've had a long day,
And now to bed we must away.
Tis midnight, and the bells do chime.
Dear friends, it's almost fairy time!"
The couples retired to their rooms above,
Wrapped in the sweetness of their love.

Rivers of happiness flow down their cheeks and rush to the floor forming a pool of joy and delight. Love sparkels in the air making everything aglow. They have married their dreams and are brimming with new hopes for the future. A new life has begun.

Katie Besworth (age 8)

Callyn Vandersleen (age 9)

Enchanting music filled the halls;
Gentle notes echoed through the walls.
"Hand in hand with fairy grace,
Will we sing and bless this place.
Now until the break of day,
Through this house each fairy stray,
So shall all the couples three,
Ever true in loving be.
Trip away, make no stay;
Meet me all by break of day."

Anika Johnson (age 8)